C000231826

Liana,

All the Best.

Nina, Dan, Jim & Ollie

7th October 2022

WILD ABOUT
Clapham

MORE THAN JUST A COMMON

By Andrew Wilson

Sponsored by

LONDON REALTY

For my Mum, Ann Wilson, who sadly passed away whilst I was working on this book.
She was a great supporter of what I do and would always eagerly await my latest project.

Clockwise from top left: Holy Trinity Church, The New Library on the High Street, The Bandstand and Cedars Terraces as viewed from across The Common. **Previous page:** Holy Trinity Church at night.

Contents

Welcome to Wild About Clapham

Welcome to my latest book on Clapham, the 17th book in my ever expanding series on the villages and towns of South West London.

Clapham has been on my list of places to do for some while, ever since I was invited into the area five years ago by a company on Northcote Road to do a book on Battersea. As you will know, Clapham Common is shared by both places and as I discovered then and was reminded of when researching this book, the Common was for ever being fought over for grazing rights. Amazingly, the sheep were still here up until the First World War, although I believe the fighting over rights etc. had stopped many years before. You also share that other local marvel, The Bandstand, which is such a lovely feature of the Common and wonderful to photograph.

As with all my projects, there are many people to thank for their help along the way. Firstly, Alyson Wilson (good name that but no relation), Derrick Johnson and Peter Jefferson Smith from The Clapham Society. They kindly provided me with a short history of the area and also helped with much of the background to accompany the pictures. Being primarily a photographer, I very selfishly think it is mostly all about the pictures but of course from a readers perspective, the words are equally as important. So a huge thanks to them, as they saved me a lot of effort. They also had a great source of old pictures, which I always feel is fun to insert to remind people what things used to be like. I am also extremely grateful to Roger, Marcus and Sophie Williams from London Realty, who are behind the new development south of the Common next to Lambeth College, Thornton Park, and who kindly agreed to sponsor my book. I have been working with them for some years now but this is by far our biggest project to date.

During the 18 months or so that I have been working on this project, I have met numerous people and visited many places and although far too many to mention in person, I am extremely grateful for their help and for giving me permission to enter and take some pictures, without which this would not be the book that it is. I would also like to thank my new designer, Matt Inman from Spinning Top, who I worked with some years ago and it has been fun to catch up after all these years. I should also mention, Paul Sherfield, who is my colour consultant, who continues to ensure that the pictures that I take appear wondrously on the pages of my books.

I have come to photography quite late in my life and pinch myself every time that I am out with my camera that this is work, how lucky am I. People say to me that the sun is always shining in my books, which is wonderful and something I spend many hours striving for. I hope you enjoy my latest book and if you have a moment please let me know what you think or perhaps follow me on social media – @WildLondonPics

Andrew Wilson,
September 2018

Left: My lovely springer spaniel, Josie, has been on all of my photographic journeys ever since I started this series of books 8 years ago, here she is taking a drink on Long Pond. Sadly, she's now a little elderly and less spritely on her feet and finds it hard to keep up, so accompanies me less and less these days, which is a shame.

Opposite: An icy late afternoon on Long Pond.

Clapham

A SHORT HISTORY OF CLAPHAM
by Peter Jefferson Smith of The Clapham Society

History first mentions Clapham in 871. It stood on a hilltop looking north onto the road from London to the south-west; to the south-east ran the old Roman Stane Street. Off the main roads, the centuries passed in obscurity. Then, in the sixteenth century, rich Londoners began discovering the village.

There was an old Manor House next to the little church. Bartholomew Clerke, a courtier and diplomat, turned it into a great mansion, where he invited amongst others Queen Elizabeth I to dine. After him, the manor was bought by Henry Atkins, court physician to James I. From about the 1630s, London merchants built their "retiring houses" here. Most of them Puritans in religion, they were viewed with suspicion by the authorities, who described Clapham as a "Whig warren". The greatest of the new houses became the home of Will Hewer, trading partner of the diarist Samuel Pepys, who died here in 1703.

With this new interest in the area, the village expanded through Old Town and southwards. During the eighteenth century, the Common became surrounded by large houses with spacious gardens. Most of these have been redeveloped, but some remain on North and West Side. The Common itself remained rough ground prone to flooding – "little better than a morass", claimed one travel writer. Highwaymen and thieves abounded. On one of the ponds, Benjamin Franklin experimented with oil on troubled water, having been introduced to the phenomenon on his way to England in 1757. In the latter part of the century, residents began to level and drain the ground, as well as plant trees, making the Common increasingly like a leisure park.

The old Parish Church was now ill-situated and obsolete. In 1776 the parishioners led by John Thornton built a new church (Holy Trinity) on the Common. Seating over 1,000, it was soon filled by a congregation eager to hear the preaching of John Venn. He was part of a group known to history as the Clapham Sect – evangelicals determined not just to spread their faith, but also to root out evils from society. First and worst was the Atlantic slave trade. Championed in Parliament by

Above: The Pavement in the early 1900s from the roof of Holy Trinity Church. This and all the old pictures of Clapham featured within this book have been provided by The Clapham Society.

William Wilberforce, in 1807 they secured the abolition of the trade.

When the first census was taken in 1801, the parish had 5,000 inhabitants. By 1901, this had risen tenfold; the detached and exclusive village became part of the sprawling metropolis. The enabler of change was public transport: from the 1820s, regular coach services took the man of affairs to his City office; from 1870, horse drawn trams could take the artisan; and in 1900, the underground arrived.

Up to the 1870s, developers continued to

Above: Clapham Cross c1910.

build large detached or semi-detached villas for the rich. Crescent Grove and Grafton Square were urban enclaves in what were still, just about, rural surroundings. In 1825, the great developer Thomas Cubitt started to build on the Clapham Park estate. Smaller terraces were built for the many tradespeople who supplied the material needs of the village, while other needs were met by new churches, chapels and schools. Exclusivity was maintained by fending off the railway companies, who took the name Clapham to their junction in Battersea.

Then and now: Clapham South Side circa 1900 and today. Notice that the milestone has moved since the original picture was taken.

Among the last of these developments were the massive terraces facing the Common and flanking Cedars Road. Apart from these and a few other streets of large houses leading off the Common, developers now turned to squeezing smaller terraces onto small plots on infill land. The Common might well have come under attack, had it not been for a London-wide movement which enabled Commons to be purchased and cared for by the public authorities. In 1877 Clapham Common came under their care, becoming ever more like a municipal park, complete with its magnificent 1890 bandstand.

By the time of the First World War, the character of Clapham had changed. Once the retreat of intellectuals and professionals, such as the architect Sir Charles Barry, it was now the home of lower City workers. To aesthetes it had become a bit of a joke, but to the judiciary, who defined the "reasonable man" as "the man on the Clapham Omnibus", it epitomised solid respectability. It maintained this character right through the inter-war years. When Noel Coward came to celebrate "This Happy Breed", his subjects were a lower-middle class family living in Clapham.

The inter-war years were a time of decline. Those with the means to do so moved out

Above: There were quite a few of the shelters built during the war, thankfully they got limited use, as the war came to an end. Besides Growing Underground, they have also been used for document storage and more topically, in 1948, Baron Baker, a local West Indian concerned about the welfare of immigrants, arranged for those arriving from Jamaica on the SS Empire Windrush to be accommodated in the Clapham South shelter (above). They found jobs through the nearest Labour Exchanges in Brixton and Tooting, thus forming the basis of the multi-racial community we have today.

to the new commuter suburbs, linked to the capital by electric train services and the extension of the Northern Line. The High Street became shabby. Much of the new building was driven by the local councils replacing worn out property, a trend which intensified after the damage of the Second World War.

In both World Wars, much of the Common was given over to allotments, and in the Second, an anti-aircraft battery occupied the space now used for events. Deep shelters were dug under the tube line. The one at Clapham South was used after the War for emergency accommodation, most famously in 1948 for Jamaicans arriving on the Empire Windrush. More recently, the tunnels near Clapham Common have been leased by an enterprising company called Growing Underground.

Change came with the swinging sixties. The baby boomers forsook their parents' suburbs for the metropolitan life of what some called "South Chelsea". Redevelopment by the Council was halted first by local resistance groups and later by Government policies. The Picture House opened in Venn Street. At The Pavement, a greasy spoon café became a posh deli, later a picture framer and gallery, and most recently an independent bookshop. The modest

Below: During the war, part of the Common was turned over to growing vegetables.

Above: Growing Underground, led by their founder Richard Ballard (pictured) started using the unoccupied underground tunnels off Clapham High Street in 2015 and grow a variety of salad items from fennel to peas. The growing cycle is controlled by special lighting, hence the pink hue and they have been so successful that they are looking to expand.

houses of Victorian bank clerks became the stunning homes of bankers. The baby boomers prospered, but the effect on prices meant that their millennial children became generation rent. But they still had the means to enjoy the vibrant night life of the High Street.

Post-millennial Clapham is well pictured in John Lanchester's Capital (2012). He assembles a range of characters in his fictitious Pepys Road: the wealthy banker who gets his come-uppance in the 2008 crash, his spendthrift wife, her Polish builder, the old lady who has lived there most of her life, the football prodigy, the illegal immigrant working as a traffic warden, and the Asian family in the corner shop – a picture of our Clapham today.

The Clapham Society aims to help improve the quality of life in Clapham and to strengthen its sense of community. We seek to promote excellence in new developments as well as conservation of the best features of the past, and we are consulted on current planning and development proposals.

We want **Clapham** to be a vibrant, exciting and safe place to live, with job opportunities and good shopping and leisure. The Society organises a programme of meetings about matters of local and/or current interest, we lead guided walks around the area, and we circulate a monthly newsletter to members.

For details go to claphamsociety.com.

The Clapham Society

Then and now: The Fountain circa 1900 and today. Notice how the trees now almost obscure St Mary's in the background. Unfortunately it wasn't possible to stand exactly where the original was taken as there is now a large tree in the way.

Below: The anti-aircraft battery placed on the Common during the war, you can just make out Cedars Terraces in the background to the left.

Then and now: The Clock Tower in the early 1900s and today. Notice that in those days the tube station entrance was on the other side of the road (on the left, not shown).

Clapham Old Town

The curved road named 'The Pavement', which lines The Common perpendicular to Clapham High Street, leads north into the quaint Old Town. The last few great country villas, first erected in the late seventeenth century, still decorate the streets here and contrast with the Victorian terraces of other areas of Clapham. An abundance of cafes, pubs and bars, clustered around The Common and up through central Old Town, create a hub of activity whether this be a morning coffee meeting in Madeleine, a trip to Moen Butchers, a meal at The Dairy or a Friday night cocktail in No. 32. These streets and the elegant homes of adjacent roads have housed some famous faces over the years, including the architect of Westminster Cathedral, John Francis Bentley, and fierce abolitionist and one of the founders of London University, Zachary Macaulay.

Opposite: The Pavement today and above, in 1973. The Deane & Co building, now Sass & Belle, is the finest surviving Clapham shop, originally built as a grocer's and taken over in 1837 by Henry Deane, a Chemist. A fine looking building, it's amazing that his sign still survives and of more interest to the author of this book, he turns out to have been a keen photographer and is responsible for the earliest photographic record of the area. **Overleaf:** The Pavement in early autumn and people out enjoying the last days of warm sunshine.

Above: The Dairy was opened by Robin and Sarah Gill in March 2013 and they obviously like the area, as this is one of three places they run locally. They also own Counter Culture, which is next door and Sorella, which is in Clapham Manor Street.

Above top left: The Sun pub in Old Town, which dates from 1880, when it replaced a previous inn that stood here.

Above middle and bottom: M Moen & Sons the butchers, who have been on The Pavement for over 20 years.

Above top right: The Fire Crew were out again entertaining the children at this year's Old Town Fair.

Bottom right: Counter Culture and The Diary.

Below top left: Maritime House in Old Town was built just before WW2 for the National Union of Seamen, hence the dolphins adorning the top of the building and sits on the site of the old Clapham Hall. Since the 1990s, when they moved out, it's mostly been converted into flats.

Below middle left: The beautiful row of Queen Anne houses' in Old Town.

Below bottom left: The Cattle Trough at the end of The Pavement up near Clapham Common Tube station.

Below top right: Pond Framing and Clapham Books on The Pavement. Before the bookshop moved here from the High Street to join the framers in April 2014, there was a gallery here.

Below bottom right: No32 on The Pavement. There has been a drinking establishment here for almost 300 years, starting out in 1722 as The Cock Tavern.

Inset top: Sass and Belle on The Pavement.

This page: Trinity Restaurant in The Polygon opened in 2006; run by Adam Byatt, who started his food loving career at Claridges at the age of 16, has since moving to Clapham earned himself a Michelin Star.

This page top: The Polygon.

Bottom left and right: Up until recently, this was the Experian Building but they have moved out and this large block on North Side is to be turned over to residential use. It was built in 1917 by the Ross Company, who amongst other things produced lenses for guns (they had to rapidly expand in WW1 to help the war effort). For the first 60 years of the last century Ross were the UK's leading manufacturer of lenses, binoculars, telescopes and scientific instruments. Sadly, they merged with another company and their name disappeared, with manufacturing ceasing in Clapham in 1975.

This page: Omnibus Theatre on North Side was opened in 2013 after a lengthy campaign by a group of local people to save what used to be the old Clapham Library. A great amenity for local people, it now plays host to a multitude of events,including back in May 2018 a book festival.

The Common By The Pavement

In olden times, it was the topography that made Clapham an ideal place in which to settle. It was the first high ground above the Thames flood plain to the south of London. The 220 acres of grass and woodland lie on a plateau formed by a layer of gravel overlying clay. As with much common land, for hundreds of years grazing rights on the Common were regularly fought over by the locals. It wasn't until the 1800s that things settled down, although grazing did still continue up until the start of WW1.

Inset: One of the lions surrounding the fountain.

Main picture: the Drinking Fountain was cast in bronze in 1884 and depicts a woman giving water to a beggar. Erected by the United Kingdom Temperance and General Provident Institution on the northern approach to London Bridge, it was moved here in 1895 when its weight began to crack the bridge approach.

Holy Trinity On The Common

Holy Trinity Church was built in the late eighteenth century to replace the old Parish Church, which became too small for the population of a fast growing Clapham. It opened in 1776 and was frequented by The Clapham Sect. At the core of the group of friends was Henry Thornton, son of one of the wealthiest merchants in Europe residing in Clapham, William Wilberforce and Zachary Macaulay. All men were strongly religious and devoted their lives to social and humanitarian causes such as education and bible translation, at home and overseas. Most famously, William Wilberforce figure headed the abolition of the slave trade in 1807.

Clapham Common Across The Seasons

Since the days when it served as grazing land for the Manors of Clapham and Battersea, the rights to Clapham Common have been fought over fiercely. Even today, despite being under complete ownership of Lambeth Council, a walk across the Common from east to west will mean crossing the Borough boundary between Wandsworth and Lambeth. Whilst grazing continued until as late as the 1920s, this huge triangular expanse of land has served many functions.

Its gravel has been exploited for road making, pits later becoming ponds. During the War Years, it was used for allotments, trench building practise and air-raid shelters. It has gradually progressed from wasteland and the site of petty crime into a true park and place for leisure, secured in the 1870s when under threat from developers. By the late nineteenth century, an Avenue, Bandstand and Speaker's Corner were in use. During the mid-twentieth century, The Greater London Horse Show was held here and more recently, pop concerts. Nowadays, at least 15 sports utilise this space, including cricket, frisbee, fishing, lacrosse and Australian Rules.

CLAPHAM CHURCH LOOKING EAST.
Published by H N Batten Clapham Common. 1827.

Above: Across the Common towards Holy Trinity Church, a painting by T M Baynes 1827.

Clockwise from top left: Feeding the geese on Long Pond, The Common by The Pavement during the big freeze of February 2018, Clapham Common West and The Bandstand.

The Common in Autumn

Opposite Page: Clapham Common West and St Barnabas Church. Erected in 1898, St Barnabas was built in the grounds of a large and beautiful 18th century mansion called The Shrubbery, which originally had a frontage onto the Common.

This page:

Top and bottom left: Windmill Drive.

Middle left: Common West.

Top right: The main Common by The Bandstand.

Bottom right: The Common by Holy Trinity Church.

The Common in Fog

This page clockwise from top left: Pigeons beside Holy Trinity Church, The Bandstand, the lone tree on the main Common and the playground on Common West.

Overleaf: Mount Pond.

The Common in Winter

The Beast from the East

In late February 2018, the UK was struck by a mighty cold spell all the way from Siberia, which soon came to be known as The Beast from the East.

Opposite page: Long Pond.

This page, clockwise from top left: Omnibus Theatre North Side, Common West, North Side and children making their way to school across the main Common.

Overleaf: Common West.

This page: Top left: The paddling pool beside Holy Trinity Church. The other three pictures are from the main Common. **Opposite:** The Bandstand.

The Common in Spring

This page: Spring flowers. **Overleaf:** the beautiful Common Blue butterfly.

The Common in Summer

After such a cold winter, followed by a late spring, the UK has then gone onto break all records for the hottest summer since records began in 1910. No wonder the English glory in talking endlessly about the weather.

Top right: Large Skipper butterfly.

Middle: Canada geese beside Long Pond.

Bottom: Common West Side.

Overleaf:

Top right: The lone tree in the middle of the main Common.

Middle: Cooling down with an ice cream on the Common beside The Pavement.

Bottom: The paddling pool beside Holy Trinity Church got a lot of use this summer.

Wild Flower Meadow

In November 2017 the TLE (Trees,Landscape and Ecology) Sub Group of CCMAC (Clapham Common Management Advisory Committee) successfully applied to the Mayor of London's Greener City Fund for a grant to plant a wild flower Meadow on Clapham Common. The project started in February of 2018 with the help of numerous local volunteers as well as regular support from GoodGym who cut 6 large strips of turf to leave areas of soil that were both seeded and planted with wild flower plugs to create a wild flower haven that started flowering in June. Very quickly the flowers attracted pollinators previously rarely seen on the Common including Purple Hairstreak and Painted Lady butterflies (inset opposite page) as well as many different species of bee. With 2018 being the hottest summer on record, watering the wildflowers became a huge challenge but with almost daily volunteer sessions the flowers not only survived but thrived and it is hoped will now naturally spread to other parts of the common.

Main image left to right:
Adrian Darley, Zach Daschler-Dawson, June Dawson, Jo Darley, Nicky Kersley, Rachel Harris and as volunteers we don't always take names on the day and we sadly don't know who the lady on the far right is.

A walk around Clapham Old Town

WHICH WILL TAKE YOU AROUND
1½ HOURS DEPENDING ON HOW
TEMPTED YOU ARE BY THE DETOURS.

———

Start at Clapham Common Underground Station.

1. The Underground reached Clapham Common in 1900. The present station is by Charles Holden, built in 1924 when the line was extended to Morden. The Clock Tower was a gift in 1906 from a Mayor of Wandsworth, the borough which then included Clapham. The half-timbered pub opposite, once The Plough, is actually a coaching inn of 1816 behind a mock Tudor refront of 1928. Over Waitrose (No. 5 The Pavement), a plaque to the Macaulay family, philanthropic campaigners. The triangle of open space, part of the Common, has recently been improved by removal of railings. The mounds cover Second World War air raid shelters. Cross to The Pavement by the pedestrian controlled lights, and continue walking with the shops to your right.

2. In the row of mostly 19th century shops, the finest is No. 17, built in 1824, and a chemist's for 150 years. The name Deane & Co can still be seen on the upper side wall.

3. After two blocks of 1930s flats and opposite a pub, the old Fire Station (1868) is a rare survivor of the early years of the London Fire Brigade. Its former use is recorded by one of the Society's green plaques, others of which will be seen elsewhere on this walk. The pub on your right was once The Cock, and a pub has been here since at least the 18th century. Wingate Square, is named after the proprietor of a nearby 19th century grocery. On the other side of the road is The Polygon, built in 1792 but extensively rebuilt after Second World War damage. On the corner, No. 1 The Polygon, currently an estate agent, has a 19th century grocer's shopfront with oil jars. Beyond The Polygon, the large open space, once given over wholly to buses, was landscaped in 2014 to create an urban piazza – this will be seen on the return journey. We now detour away from Old Town. Turn right just before the Sun PH, into Grafton Square, and walk round the square.

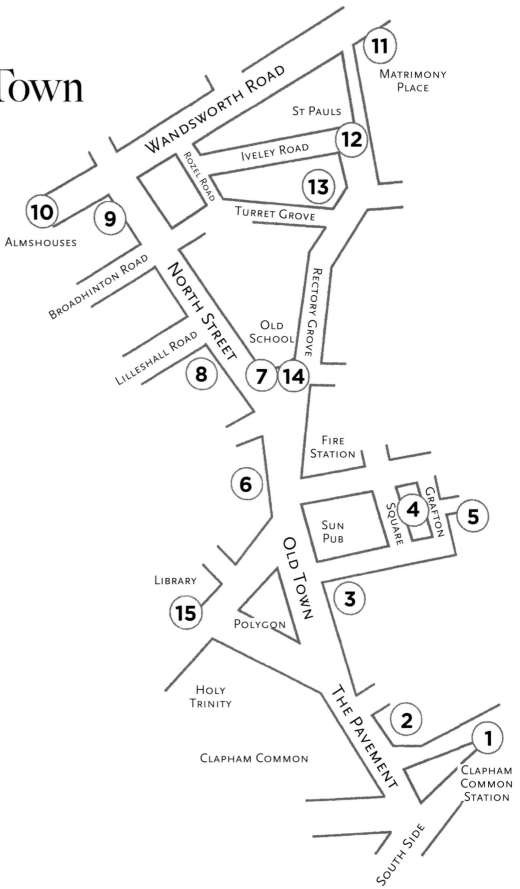

Clockwise from top left: Clapham Common Station, The Old Fire Station, The former People's Church off Grafton Square, Broadhinton Road, Hibberts' Almshouses and Sycamore House.

4. Grafton Square was developed in 1846-51 by an Irish militia Captain, Thomas Ross. The smaller houses, Nos. 1-3, were there when he started, and Ross incorporated them in his scheme. He built the tall flamboyant terraces, round a central garden, more typical of Kensington than Clapham.

5. At the far side of the square, by a red pillar box, Belmont Road leads to Clapham Manor School. It is worth a detour to the ultra-modern extension to the school, by architects dRMM, shortlisted for the Stirling Prize in 2010. Leave the square by the road passing a former church, walk to Old Town and there turn right. The former People's Church, in the north-west corner of Grafton Square, is an imposing classical building of 1882-9, altered c1910, and converted in 2007 into housing.

6. Over the shops on the other side of Old Town, there is a coat of arms with the motto "Contentment passe richesse" said to have come from the former Manor House. This part of Old Town has fine Georgian houses of the 1780s. No.23, on your right just past the Fire Station, has good Grade II listed railings. Sycamore House, opposite, a grand house set back from the road, was once the main office of a grand laundry with Royal appointments. Cross Old Town, and where the road forks, bear left into North Street.

7. The old school building, now the City Learning Centre, is described on the return journey. Continue along North Street to the junction with Lillieshall Road.

8. Around this junction is a pretty cluster of terraces and cottages, the terraces of the 1830s and the cottages (Grade II listed) about 1827-29. This part of Lillieshall Road was then Orchard Street, and it ended at the village Cricket Ground. The Bobbin, a small but elaborate pub of 1887, is named after Tim Bobbin, an 18th century caricaturist and writer of humorous pieces in Lancashire dialect. At Broadhinton Road, it is worth another short detour to look at two rows of pretty terraced houses, all 1863. At the end of North Street, turn left at the lights.

9. Here is a large flamboyant pub (1876), currently closed. This was once the Nag's Head, replacing a much older pub of the same name – North Street was originally Nag's Head Lane. Opposite, the Plough Brewery, now offices, was

Clockwise from top left: Eden Community Garden, St Paul's Church, Rectory Grove, Rectory Grove houses 20-28, Hope House and Matrimony Place

built about 1870, replacing an older brewery, at one end of a terrace called Brewhouse Buildings (c.1810). A detour to your left along Wandsworth Road brings you to the Hibbert almshouses.

10. The almshouses were founded in 1859 by two sisters, the last Clapham members of the Hibbert family. The Hibberts' fortune came from slave plantations in Jamaica, and George Hibbert MP, uncle of the founders, was one of Wilberforce's leading opponents. Return to the traffic lights and continue along Wandsworth Road, until you reach a row of shops on your right. But please note that there will be some steps; if that will be difficult for you, turn right into Rozel Road and left into Iveley Road, at the end of which you re-join the route at 12.

Unhistoric it may feel, but Wandsworth Road is the ancient route from London to West Surrey and Hampshire. On the far side of the

road is the steep roof of Heathbrook School, (1886). The Westbury Estate, built by the GLC in 1964-7, has two tower blocks of the sort that Clapham escaped. After the shops, just before the pedestrian crossing, you pass an alley on your right (Matrimony Place).

11. A little beyond the entrance to Matrimony Place, No. 575 was the house of Khadambe Asalache, a Kenyan poet, economist and UK civil servant, who filled it with his carvings. He bequeathed it to the National Trust, which now opens it to the public (as it is very small, prior booking is essential). Turn into Matrimony Place and walk up the steps to St. Paul's Churchyard. As you walk up the steps, traffic noise gives way to birdsong, and you reach the ancient churchyard of Clapham, now largely cleared of gravestones. The eastern side has been laid out as the Eden Community Garden. St

Paul's Church, built in 1815, extended in 1879, occupies the site of the medieval parish church, demolished when a new church was built on the Common. If the church is open, go inside to see the late 17th century Atkins monuments in the Lady Chapel and the memorial to William Hewer over the Lady Chapel door. In front of the church, there is a small square, part of Rectory Grove.

12. This is the oldest part of Clapham. To your right, Nos. 8-10 Rectory Grove have handsome frontages of about 1800. Either at No. 8 or on a house previously on the site, Zachary Macaulay set up an African Academy to educate the sons of African families from Sierra Leone. The buildings to your left, adjoining No. 2A, Ingleton House, were the hall and chapel for a boys' home from 1912 to 1938. The chapel (No. 2A) is now Clapham Pottery. In Rectory Grove, go to the right, to the junction with Turret Grove.

Clockwise from top right: Maritime House, Holy Trinity Church and the new Oasis shop and the fine row of Queen Anne houses in Old Town.

13. The Elizabethan Manor House stood here. Demolished in 1837, after which the attractive villas in Turret Grove were built, its turret gave the name to the street. In Rectory Grove, Cromwell Cottages (Nos. 20-28) date from 1838. The winding Rectory Grove was the main street of the old village, originally called just "The Street". Hope House c.1790, has door surrounds of Coade stone, an artificial stone manufactured on the South Bank. There are other large houses of the mid-19th century. The Rectory Gardens cottages are on the site of the former Holy Trinity Rectory.

14. The Victorian school building on your right is the former parochial school; a school has been on this site since at least 1648. The old building has been imaginatively adapted to house Lambeth's City Learning Centre. After the City Learning Centre, cross over to the right-hand side of Old Town. The houses you now pass were described earlier in the walk. Across the road and to your left, after the Fire Station (1964) comes Maritime House, built as a seamen's union headquarters in 1939, hence the dolphins and ship's prow aloft. Next, Nos. 39-43, fine houses of 1706 (blue plaque to JF Bentley, the architect of Westminster Cathedral). No. 45 (Oasis shop), built about 1690, is believed to be the oldest building in Clapham. Leaving the piazza to your left, walk to the road junction outside Omnibus.

15. Omnibus was built in 1889 as Clapham Library. In 2012, a new library was opened in Clapham High Street, and the old building was taken over by a locally formed trust, which has transformed it into an arts centre. Outside it is a Roman memorial stone, now illegible, which came here via Cavendish House on South Side, but was earlier in the Tower of London. Nearby on the Common, is Holy Trinity Church, built in 1774-6 as the new Parish Church for Clapham, and extended in 1903. It is associated with the Clapham Sect, religious and philanthropic campaigners. This is the start of Clapham Common North Side, a walk in itself (Clapham Walk No. 7). To conclude the present walk, cross the road to go back along the edge of the Common to the Underground

This walk was devised by The Clapham Society, who have kindly allowed us to feature it. The Clapham Society is a local civic amenity society, which aims to improve the quality of life for residents, promote quality in new developments and to conserve the best features of the past. For further information please visit claphamsociety.com.

Street Scenes

Even before the establishment of the Saxon village Clopeham, meaning village (ham) by the short hill (clopp), the Roman military road Stane Street, known as South Side today, ran over this land to connect London with Chichester. In medieval times, despite the population explosion, famine and The Black Death halted expansion, once farmed land became woodland. John Rocque's 1745 Map of the County of Surrey shows the road to the north, now known as Wandsworth Road, connecting the village with the rest of Surrey.

The great manors built by incoming wealthy inhabitants in the seventeenth century were sadly all demolished, but reminders of Clapham's history and residents are found everywhere. For example, Macaulay Road is named named after the Macaulay family, who were a well known local family back in the 19th century, Zachary Macaulay being part of The Clapham Sect. Furthermore, Clapham boasts one of the highest concentrations of blue plaques seen anywhere in London.

The oldest standing buildings date to the early eighteenth century, meaning that a variety of period styles characterise Clapham's streets today: Queen Anne, Georgian, Regency and Victorian. Street scenes changed most drastically during the nineteenth century, where the railway encouraged a ten-fold increase in Clapham's population, and people once travelling by foot, horseback or coach, travelled by tram, tube and even at the turn of the century, the motor car.

Above: this clever map shows by the use of an overlay how the streets along South Side were formed out of the large estates that used to be here in the early 19th century. Opposite: The Clock Tower. Erected in 1906, the Tower was originally situated further west, but was moved when the adjacent station entrances were redesigned. There is a large plaque at its base commemorating its donor, Alexander Glegg, who was the Mayor of Wandsworth 1905-06.

Abbeville Road

The little enclave of shops along Abbeville Road appeared at the end of the 19th century to cater for the new streets that were springing up along the South Side, as the big houses were broken up and sold for redevelopment (see map on the previous page).

Top right: A monkey in the window of Grand Passion.

Abbeville Road

FÊTE

Founded in 1997 and held every summer since, Abbeville Fête, has grown to be one of the biggest in the area, with over 100 stalls and over 5,000 visitors. Great fun for the locals as well as visitors, the organizers also raise a lot of money for charity.

Belmont Road and Close

Top left: Oddfellows Hall in Belmont Close was built in 1852 as a chapel.

Top right and bottom left: Clapham Manor School. Formerly Stonhouse Street School, there has been a school on this site since the 1840's. Amongst the buildings, there is a rather impressive new block (pictured).

Bottom right: part of the Clapham Manor Estate in Belmont Close; built in the 1970s, all the houses are low-rise and the area is pedestrianised.

Broomwood Road

This page: Named after Broomwood House, formerly Broomfield, and the home of William Wilberforce, during his successful campaign to abolish the slave trade. The road is aligned with the carriage drive to his house.

The building of Thomas's Preparatory School dates from 1882. A rather striking building with its twin circular staircase towers, which are visible from quite a distance, it was originally the County Secondary School for Girls, and from 1976 Walsingham School. The building became redundant after the reorganization of the education system and in the late 1980s, after a period of uncetainty became a private school, as it is today.

Clapham Common North Side
THE CEDARS TERRACES

A prominent landmark of Clapham are the French Renaissance style Cedars Terraces, where Cedars Road meets North Side, which can be seen from the opposite side of the Common. They were originally designed to be the entrance to a major development called Park Town, envisioned by their architect J T Knowles junior. The build was cut short, partly because the railway crossing the land was deemed an eyesore. Each terrace contains five houses, with the end houses having an extra roof pavilion, and they have served as flats and a hostel. Exquisite detail to window heads and balconies remains preserved, equally preserved by other Knowles homes on Cedars Road. No 47 at the end of the eastern terrace was home to Edvard Grieg's London Agent, a music publisher named George Augener. Consequently, Clapham was visited many times by the Norwegian composer and pianist, along with his wife, during the nineteenth century. Their visits were commemorated by flying the Norwegian flag from the house; nowadays they are commemorated by a Blue Plaque.

Clapham Common North Side

Opposite top left: The Elms, now part of Royal Trinity Hospice, dates from 1754.

This page: Church Buildings date from 1714-20 and were saved from demolition in 1913, when the 199 year leases ran out, by the intervention of WW1. The scheme having been abandoned, in the 1930's the derelict houses were saved from a speculator and sold to be restored by their new owners. Sadly, the last four houses had already been demolished and are now a block of flats, see opposite page top right.

Clapham Common North Side

ROYAL TRINITY HOSPICE

Formerly the Hostel of God, it was founded in 1891 as the 'Free Home for the Dying'. From 1977 major alterations were carried out to upgrade the buildings, when the hospice, previously run by nuns, was reorganised under a lay council.

The magnificent gardens at the rear of the hospice were restored in 1981 and regularly opened to the public. Of particular note, on the large ovoid pond are four rotating squares by George Rickey, created in 1984 (pictured on the previous page). Opened in June 2018 as part of the Open Gardens Scheme, there was a huge number of mating blue damselflies to be seen on the pond.

Clapham Common South Side

Main picture: The Orangery as seen from one of the balconies on the Notre Dame Estate. Dating from 1793, it was described in a sale document of 1810 as 'an extremely elegant and costly Greenhouse built of Portland Stone'. Not in the best of repair, there are plans to upgrade the rather elegant building as part of the new development next to Lambeth College, 'Thornton Park'.

Top left: Lambeth College opened in 1993, using the space formerly known as the Henry Thornton Boys Secondary School.

This Page: Clapham South Station on the Northern Line opened in 1926 as part of the Morden extension of what was then known as The City and South London Railway.

Opposite Top: Many of the larger houses and villas along Southside have become hotels.

Opposite bottom left and right: The former South London Hospital for Women, opposite Clapham South Tube Station, which closed in 1984 is now a Tesco.

THE SOUTH LONDON HOSPITAL FOR WOMEN
(INCORPORATED)
FOUNDED A.D. 1912.
THIS BUILDING WAS OPENED BY
HER MAJESTY, QUEEN MARY,
ON THE FOURTH DAY OF JULY A.D. 1916

Clapham Common West Side

Opposite page: Hightrees House was built in the 1930s on the site of a former villa of the same name.

This page:

Bottom left: The café beside the tennis courts and bowling green.

Top left: No 85 West Side. Formerly Heathview, it dates from 1856.

This page:

Inset: The flat tarmac areas that can be seen on the Common West Side are the visible remains of the low level air-raid shelters that were built during WW2 to help try and protect the local population.

Top left: One of the few remaining boundary markers found along West Side.

Top right: The bowling club.

Bottom left: No 82 West Side, a beautifully restored house with a magnificent rear garden, it was the venue for the 2018 Friends of Clapham Common summer party (see page 182).

Bottom right: Many of the houses along West Side retain the rather splendid tiles by their front doors.

Clapham Manor Street

Clapham Manor Street is one of the earlier parts of Clapham to be developed and appears on a map of 1827. Number 42 (picture below top right) dates from 1850-54 and after a period of neglect and a fire it was fully restored in 1992 and now houses the London Russian Ballet School.

Clapham High Street

Like many shopping streets, the overall look of the High Street took shape during the early 19th century, where shops were built over the front gardens of the large houses, with shops being built this way from the 1830s onwards. Towards the end of the century Clapham started to get the large shop buildings of red brick and stone which typify so many suburban shopping streets. Through a mix of replacement buildings due to war damage and regular redevelopment, some buildings of note survive, notably the former Majestic cinema and the former Temperance Billiard Hall (pictured on the next page).

This page: Clapham Common Tube Station used to be on the opposite side of the road (on the corner of Clapham Park Road) and moved to its current location when the line was extended to Mordern. The rather distinctive dome was to help provide light for the booking hall.

Top left: The former Temperance Billiard Hall.

Middle: The former Majestic cinema.

Main picture: The Clock Tower and where The Pavement meets the High Street.

Main picture: The striking new library building was opened in 2012 and was designed by architects Studio Egret West.

Middle: The outside of the new library is not the only impressive part of this building, the inside is also quite striking.

Bottom: The old signs are slowly disappearing from our streets, this one on the high street can still be made out.

Crescent Grove

This page and the next six: Crescent Grove dates from 1825-27, and is on the site of Edward Polhill's eighteenth-century villa. Crescent Grove consists of a crescent of terraced houses opposite a row of semi-detached houses linked by their coach houses, all surrounding a central garden. All elegantly preserved, the gardens in particular are beautifully maintained by local resident Marjan Johnson.

Cubitt Terrace

Cubitt Terrace, named after the local architect, was formerly part of Stonhouse Street before the formation of Clapham Manor Estate in the 1970s cut it in half. What remains is a rather pretty row of terraced cottages with nice wooden fenced front gardens.

Edgeley Road

Edgeley Road, was formerly called Vernon Road and mainly consists of rows of mansion blocks, many displaying that sign of modern times, satellite dishes.

Elms Road

Elms Road, that runs from South Side down to Abbeville Road and beyond, is named after the grand house that used to be here.

Fitzwilliam Road

Fitzwilliam Road dates from 1865-70.

Grafton Square

This page and overleaf: The houses that stand today were built by Thomas Ross and replace an eighteenth century mansion, which was demolished in the 1840s. With stucco design such as intricate trumpet shapes around their windows, these small terraces are unique. Ross only saw completion of three sides of his project. On the south-west corner, a large Congregational Church was built in 1851. One of its ministers, a well-known preacher, was a friend of Prime Minister Gladstone who was a regular visitor to Clapham. Severe damage during the Blitz called for a new Church to be built, the one standing today. On the north-west corner, a Baptist Chapel was built in the 1800s, later becoming the People's Church, before being converted to housing. The central garden has been private lawns and a tennis club. Today, it is a public space with a playground.

Hambalt Road

In May 2018, Prince Harry married the actress Meghan Markle and as with lots of streets across the country, a few in Clapham closed to traffic and held old fashioned street parties, as here in Hambalt Road off Abbeville Road (see also pages 130-131). Rather bizarrely, your author was interviewed here by a visiting German film crew, looking for a British perspective on the wedding, so my 5 minutes of fame has ended up on German TV.

Long Road

Macaulay Road

This Page: Its unsure as to whether Macaulay Road was named after Zachary Macaulay or his son, Thomas Babington Macaulay, later Baron Macaulay, both notable locally. The road itself is a fine mix of architecture, including the old Clapham Parochial School (bottom left and middle), now in residential use and a rather smart modern block (bottom right), built by the local architect Michael Squire.

Rectory Gardens

Rectory Gardens date from 1882 and have in recent times become somewhat rundown. However, as we went to press they are under redevelopment and may yet regain something of their past glory as a picturesque, traffic free, row of cottages.

Rectory Grove

ST PAUL'S

The original parish church of Clapham on this site was demolished when Holy Trinity was built on the Common in 1774-76. This church was later built (c1815) on the initiative of the Rector of Clapham, Rev John Venn, to relieve pressure on Holy Trinity.

Rectory Grove

ST PAUL'S SUMMER FÊTE

Rectory Grove

Rectory Grove and North Street were the original village streets of old Clapham (see picture top left, where Old Town divides into two, North Street going left and Rectory Grove, right). For more information on the houses and buildings of note in Rectory Grove in particular see our walk on pages 64-67.

Royal Wedding
TREGARVON ROAD & TURRET GROVE

May 18th 2018 was marked all over London and the rest of the country with street parties to celebrate the wedding of Prince Harry and Meghan Markle and we were thankfully blessed with a beautifully sunny day. Thank you also to the lady (bottom right) who kindly offered me one of her cakes and also agreed to pose for me, excellent they were too.

St Mary's Church

St Mary's Church (Our lady of Victories) dates from 1849-51 and is considered one of the finest ecclesiastical buildings in the area. Sadly, it is the sole survivor of 'The three sisters of Clapham', the spires of the Methodist Church in the High Street and the Congregational Church in Grafton Square having been destroyed in the Second World War. The Church was built on the grounds of the mansion of Lord Teignmouth, one of the Clapham Sect, which was earlier the home of Samuel Thornton. Bottom left is the adjoining monastery.

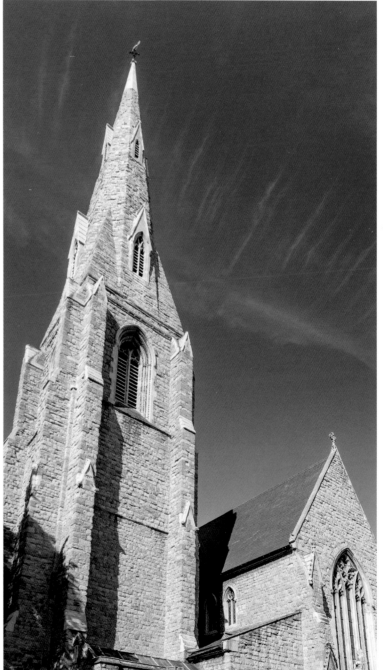

The Chase

The Chase is one of Clapham's finer roads, being wider than most and one of its oldest. Dating from mid 19th century, The Chase was originally a driveway from Wandsworth Road to the back of the mansion built in 1663 by Sir Denis Gauden, later bought by William Hewer, whose friend Samuel Pepys died there in 1703. Outside numbers 50-52 (below top right) is a fine example of a Victorian pillar box, dating from 1866, which was damaged by a car in the 1980s but carefully repaired on the insistence of the local residents. A great mix of styles, some of the houses have names over the porches.

Venn Street

The Reverend John Venn (1759-1813), after whom this street is named, was the Rector of Clapham from 1792. He was also a leader of the progressive Clapham Sect, a group of evangelical Christians who worshipped at Holy Trinity Church and who campaigned for the abolition of the slave trade amongst many other religious, philanthropic and moral causes. His grandson, Dr John Venn (1834 - 1923) invented the Venn Diagram, the art of supporting theories through the aid of diagrams, specifically three overlapping circles.

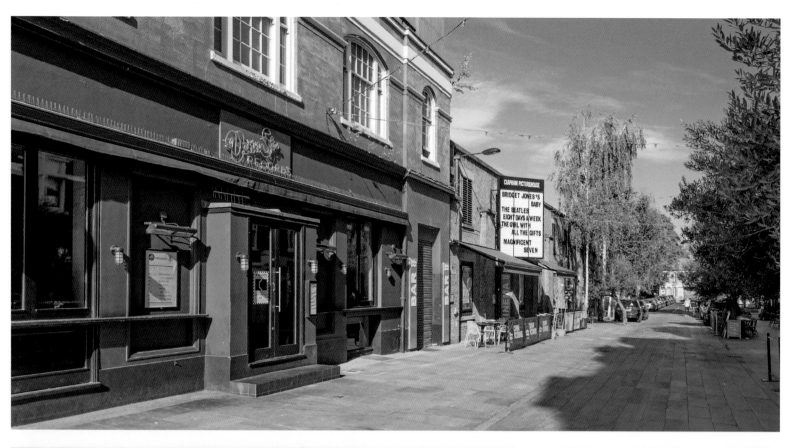

Apart from being the home to the popular local cinema, Venn Street is also the venue for a Saturday market.

Wix's Lane

Wix's Lane, which is still a footpath at the northern end, is named after Edward Wix who lived nearby in the 18th century. An ancient boundary between Clapham and Battersea, boundary markers can still be seen. Wix's Primary School, which can be found at the end of the terrace (below), was formed in 1903 and enlarged several times since and part of it is now home to Lycée Français.

Bandstand

Built in 1890, the Bandstand is the oldest and largest surviving in Greater London, and one of the largest ever built in England. In the summer of 1888 the Metropolitan Police Band gave regular concerts on Wednesday afternoons; local shops closed on these afternoons to allow assistants to 'enjoy rest and relaxation' by hearing the music. These were so popular that local residents successfully petitioned the London County Council to provide a bandstand.

The early 20th century was a great time for band concerts, with both professional bands coming in as well as the more traditional police and military bands playing. Use of the bandstand continued into the years after the Second World War. But by the 1960s and 70s traditional cast iron bandstands were thought old fashioned and by the late 1980s use of the bandstand had virtually ceased. The bandstand became derelict, and in 1997 it was put on English Heritage's Buildings at Risk Register. Aided by a massive grant from the Heritage Lottery Fund and supported by funds raised by local residents, in 2006 Lambeth Council carried out a magnificent restoration, to bring the bandstand back to how it is today and more importantly, back into use.

Above: People gather for a concert in 1912.

Bandstand

The summer of 2018 saw a series of concerts put on, which aided by the weather were very popular.

Bottom right: Beside the Bandstand is a popular little café, where chairs can be at a premium on a fine day.

Three Ponds

The 87 hectares of Clapham Common is home to three ponds, all starting life as gravel pits: Mount Pond, Eagle Pond and Long Pond. The two former ones are used to fish for carp and bream, and they are recognised for their wildlife. In 1746, with the permission of the Lord of the Manor, a banker named Henton Brown was able to divert water from Mount Pond to his house on South Side, and even build a summer-house on its island. Encroachments such as this eventually led to the formation of a Committee to protect The Common. Mount Pond also hosted scientist Benjamin Franklin's famous 'Teaspoon of oil' experiment in the eighteenth century, inspired by witnessing the calming effect of oil on sea conditions. It is believed Long Pond has been used for model boating since the mid-1800s, making it the oldest model boating site; there were periods where races were held most Saturday afternoons. Today The Clapham Model Yacht Club, running since the 1930s, organises such events most months. Long Pond was an essential source of water for London's firefighters during The Blitz. Once a fourth pond, Cock Pond is now a popular paddling pool.

Above: A watercolour of Mount Pond by Joseph Powell c1825

Long Pond

ALSO KNOWN AS THE BOATING LAKE

Top left: My companion springer, Josie, took exception to the model boat that someone was playing with and barked at it loudly.

Eagle Pond

Eagle Pond is the smallest of the three ponds found on the Common but still big enough for people to row on, which is something that went on in the early 1900s before transferring to Mount Pond. In the age of horse drawn vehicles and riding in general the ponds also served as a useful watering hole for the horses as well as the other livestock kept on the Common.

Mount Pond

The reeds around the pond are a fairly recent thing. In 1995 the council started to put together a plan for the Common, including improvements to the ponds. In order to encourage Wildlife and generally improve the condition of the water, the reed beds on Mount Pond were commissioned as part of the plans.

Sport & Leisure

Clapham has a long and rich history of sport and leisure. As early as the eighteenth century, duck-shooting, hedgehog hunting (once a popular pastime among working-class men), archery, cricket and hopping matches took place. Horse riding became restricted to a turf gallop on what is now The Avenue. Fairs were not favoured by everyone, but took place a few times a year. When the Common became the central focal point of Clapham during huge Victorian expansion, the bronze Drinking Fountain was moved here and a Bandstand was commissioned. Donkey riding and picnics were a typical Victorian family outing. Nowadays, there is a sport for everyone. Football, which really took off after Clapham Rovers won the FA Cup in 1880, caters for men, women and kids, with 5 a-side and 11 a-side games organised. With many Australian residents in Clapham, it is no surprise that The Wandsworth Demons are the most successful Aussie Rules club in England and have always practised on Clapham Common. Touch rugby takes place throughout the year and The Clapham Lacrosse Club, which welcomes all abilities, practises during summer months. Sports facilities include cricket nets, tennis courts off of Windmill drive, open every day of the week in summer, a bowling green on West Side, netball and basketball courts and a recently renovated skateboarding park. The ultimate frisbee team, Clapham Ultimate, are 11 times UK champions and practise every Monday. The famous London-Brighton cycling event, held in June each year, begins here.

Children pose for the camera beside the old Cock Pond, now the paddling pool, late 1800's.

Sports

Opposite page top: Fishing on Mount Pond.

Opposite page bottom: The exercise area on Common West.

Inset: Early morning exercise on a cold and frosty morning.

Pubs

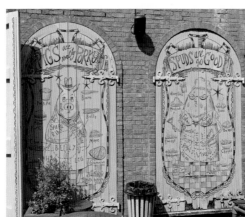

This page: Top left: Craft Beer Co, Clapham Manor Street. **Top middle and centre:** The Windmill on the Common. **Top right:** The Sun in Old Town. **Bottom right:** The Alexandra, South Side. **Bottom middle:** The Rose and Crown, The Polygon. **Bottom left:** The Railway Tavern, High Street.

This Page: Top left and middle left: The Falcon, Bedford Road. **Top middle:** The Abbeville, Abbeville Road. **Top and bottom right:** The Stonhouse, Stonhouse Street. **Middle:** The Bobbin, Lillieshall Road. **Bottom middle:** The Rookery, South Side. **Bottom left:** The Bread and Roses, Clapham Manor Street.

Street Sports

The Friends of Clapham Common

SUMMER PARTY

On the 21st June 2018 I was kindly invited by The Friends to their summer party, which was held at a fine house on West Side, with a wonderful garden. As with most evenings this past summer, we were blessed with fine weather. Chaired by Martin Read (pictured bottom left on the right of the picture), The Friends work to protect and improve the Common as an active environmental group of some 500 members. They run projects to improve the biodiversity of the Common and restore its buildings and facilities.

Festivals, Fêtes & Fun

In the autumn of 2016, The Friends of Clapham Common held an event for dogs on the Common.

Besides events such as featured here, the Common hosts a multitude of activities big and small, from a pop festival in August, to fetes and people just having fun. Many years ago my wife and I entered the London to Brighton cycle event and I see to this day it still starts on the Common. We should all be thankful for the town planners, who kindly left us so many wonderful open spaces to play in.

This page: The members of the London Fine Art Studios, based in Lavender Hill, regularly meet on the Common to paint. Group members pictured are from top right, Richard Gayner, middle, Oliver Barnes and bottom Anna Datskevich - www.londonfineartstudios.com

Bandstand Beds

This page: Bandstand Beds is a community garden just off Windmill Drive and run by volunteers. During the recent really hot spell they we kind enough to allow the Wild Flower Meadow enthusiasts to fill up their watering cans (see page 62) and at the height of the summer, they were having to fill up to 84 cans to keep their precious flowers alive. www.bandstandbeds.org.uk

Clapham Old Town Fair

This page: This is Clapham created the Old Town Fair in 2016 in partnership with Clapham Omnibus and the London Fire Brigade and it has grown each year.

PRINTS FOR SALE

If you would like any of the pictures from this book as either a framed or unframed print or a canvas, please contact the publisher at *www.wildlondon.co.uk* where all the details can be found.

This goes for any of the books from the *Wild About* series which are shown opposite.

Other books in the Wild About series

Other books in the Wild About series by Andrew Wilson are available to buy from all good book stores including some branches of WH Smith and all branches of Waterstones.

London Realty is proud to sponsor Wild About Clapham

London Realty is a development management company with a first class reputation for delivering imaginative high quality schemes across London.

We will be bringing 300 new homes and a vibrant business community to Clapham on a substantial four acre site opposite Clapham Common. Once part of the famous gardens of the 18th century merchant and politician Robert Thornton, this new project will bring a new mixed-use neighbourhood to this hugely popular part of London.

The Latin inscription on the nearby Georgian orangery translates as "Here blooms perpetual spring and summer, even in other months" and we take this as our mission!

Oakhill Park, Putney SW15

LONDON REALTY

www.londonrealty.co.uk

14 Northfields Prospect, Putney Bridge Road, London SW18 1PE

All rights reserved. No part of this publication may be reproduced, stored in any retrieval system or transmitted in any form or by any means, electronic, mechanical photocopying or otherwise without the prior permission of the copyright holders. Whilst every care has been taken in the production of this book, no responsibility can be accepted for any errors or omissions. The publishers have taken all reasonable care in compiling this work but cannot accept responsibility for the information derived from third parties, which has been reproduced in good faith.

First Edition – ©Unity Print and Publishing Limited 2018

History Consultants:
Alyson Wilson, Derrick Johnson and Peter Jefferson Smith
The Clapham Society
www.claphamsociety.com

Designed by Spinning Top (UK) Ltd
www.spinning-top.com

Proofreading: Alyson Wilson with some help from Amy Wilson (pictured right).

Printed by Page Brothers of Norwich
www.pagebros.co.uk

Bound by Green Street Bindery of Oxford. www.maltbysbookbinders.com

Colour Management by Paul Sherfield of The Missing Horse Consultancy
www.missinghorsecons.co.uk

Published by Unity Print and Publishing Limited,
18 Dungarvan Avenue,
London SW15 5QU

Tel: +44 (0)20 8487 2199
aw@unity-publishing.co.uk
www.wildlondon.co.uk

Andrew Wilson uses a Canon 6D and lenses and an iPhone 7.

Follow Andrew on Twitter: @andrewpics

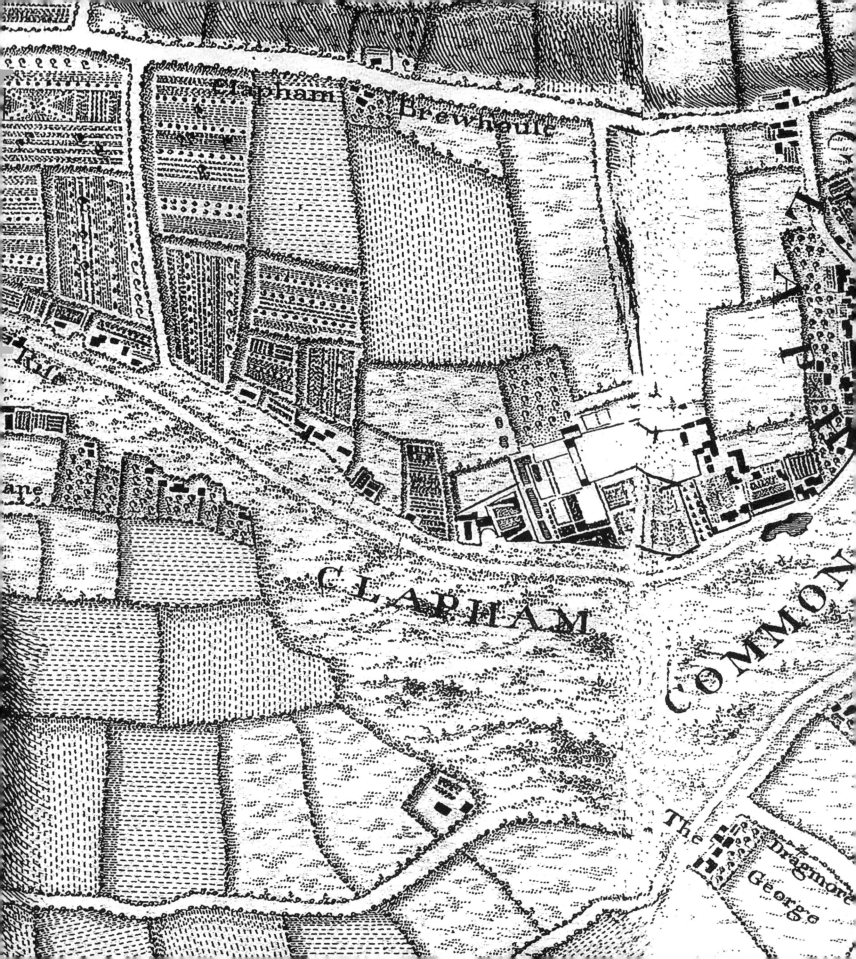

Clapham

Brewhouse

CLAPHAM

COMMON

The
Dragmore
George